To our children,

**Stephanie, Jonathan and
Debbie,**

who have challenged us
every day of their lives to
think and to re-think about
how children learn

and

In memory of our dear
friend and fellow educator,

Bernie O'Rourke

Acknowledgements

I wish to express my sincere thanks to Breda Ging, my former English teacher, now barrister and senior lecturer in law. Her dissatisfaction with traditional education led to her rather unconventional teaching style. Yet the time I spent under her "tutelage" in the nocturnal streets of Paris, the Shakespearean haunts of Stratford and the cobbled streets of Dublin was the first "real" education I ever experienced and set me thinking about what education should be.

To you, Breda, I will always be grateful.

Many thanks to all the parents who gave permission for photographs to be used in this publication. All the pictures used in this book were taken in Cherrywood Montessori School - Dublin.

Thanks to Colour Books for their help and advice.

Last, but certainly not least, many thanks to our families for their help and support throughout the years.

Contents

Maria Montessori 1

The Crucial Years 2

The Montessori Pre-school 4

The Classroom 5

The Children In The Classroom 6

The Montessori Materials 8

The Teacher 10

The Hidden Curriculum 12

Practical Life Activities. 14

Sensorial Activities 16

Mathematical Activities 18

Language Activities 20

Art, Craft And Music Activities 23

Cultural Activities 24

The Tailor Made School 26

Choosing The Right Montessori School 28

Questions Parents Ask 32

Common Criticisms Of Montessori Schools 36

We don't have to make human beings smart. They are born smart. All we have to do is stop doing the things that make them stupid.

John Holt

How Children Fail

The first Montessori school opened in 1907 in a refurbished tenement building in the slums of San Lorenzo in Italy. There were about fifty extremely underprivileged children in attendance and the staff consisted of Dr. Maria Montessori and a young untrained assistant.

Yet the success of this first Montessori school was so astounding that the Queen of Italy and many distinguished visitors from foreign countries walked through the dingy backstreets of Rome to see it with their own eyes.

During Dr. Montessori's own lifetime, her schools were opened in every continent on the globe. They started with the poor but then spread to the middle classes and the rich. Dr. Montessori wanted her schools to be for all children everywhere regardless of nationality, colour, creed or economic status.

Sadly, in recent years there has been a tendency, in some countries, for Montessori schools to place themselves out of the reach of "all children everywhere" because of increasingly high fees and selective locations. Even more unfortunate is the fact that where pre-schools are Government funded they are rarely Montessori programs.

For several years now, we have sought to provide Montessori education for "ordinary people". Through parent education classes we have tried to inform people about the benefits of this wonderful approach to child rearing, and through this short and simple book, we hope to further our aim, to put Montessori education and it's philosophy back within the reach of "all children everywhere."

Dr. Maria Montessori
1870 - 1952

"...The most important period of life is not the age of university studies, but the first one, the period from birth to the age of six. For that is the time when man's intelligence itself, his greatest implement is being formed."

Dr. Maria Montessori

The Absorbent Mind

Born in Ancona in Italy in 1870, Maria Montessori has been described by many as a woman ahead of her time, set to break the mould of traditional education.

At the age of twenty six she became Italy's first woman doctor. In the course of her medical work she began to study and to examine how children learn and how they adapt to the world they find themselves in.

At first, she worked with mentally retarded children and her outstanding success in helping these children to learn brought her acclaim and high regard throughout Europe.

In 1906 she was asked to direct the setting up of day care centres in the slums of Rome to cater for street urchins from three to six years of age. The results of this project were astonishing and out of it was born what we now call the "Montessori Method" of education.

This new approach to children and to education took root immediately and spread within a few years to every continent on the globe.

Dr. Montessori died in 1952 but her work continues to grow and expand.

Maria Montessori was a doctor, an educator, a humanitarian and a life long campaigner for the protection of children and childhood.

To her we owe a huge debt for the part she played in making the twentieth century the century of the child.

Modern psychologists have now come to accept what Dr. Maria Montessori told us a long time ago, that the first six years of life are the most crucial ones and that children under six have extraordinary minds which operate in a different way to that of the adult.

Montessori pointed out that all children under six, of every race, colour and creed have the ability to absorb knowledge, language and culture effortlessly from their surrounding environment, simply by living in it. This ability is short lived however. It is a once in a lifetime phenomenon and it disappears after the child's sixth year.

The "absorbent mind" as Montessori called it, is nature's gift to all children to enable them to adapt to the time, place, culture and traditions that they are born into.

Montessori also pointed out that all children under six go through certain temporary "phases" which she called "sensitive periods" which play a very specific role in their development.

These are short periods of time in a child's life when the child seems to experience an intense fascination for:- performing certain movements; for using all of her senses; for using language; for maintaining order and routines and for noticing small objects and minor details.

For example, many parents will have noticed their young child's temporary obsession with repeatedly going up and down steps; with touching and handling everything; with repeating words and phrases; with insisting that everything be done in a set, almost ritualistic fashion; and with insisting that every detail of a story be repeated no matter how small or seemingly insignificant.

Dr. Montessori, with her usual penetrating insight was not content just to observe these phenomena but went to great pains to understand and explain them. For example, she pointed out that the child's insistence on order is not a tantrum but a desperate attempt to clutch onto the small framework of order that she has managed to construct on this big, booming, confusing world she finds herself in.

She discovered that during these "sensitive periods" when a child is drawn to a particular activity, the child finds it easier to learn and perfect certain skills than at any other time in her life.

The crucial discovery that Montessori made and the one that is perhaps least known by adults in general is that if a child is allowed to respond to the call of her sensitive periods without being constantly interrupted and impeded by well meaning adults, a most important psychological development takes place in her personality. She becomes joyful, calm and at peace with herself.

In the Montessori pre-school the teacher takes these "sensitive periods" and the "absorbent mind" very much into consideration when preparing an environment for the child.

The Montessori Pre-school...

...A Prepared Environment

A Montessori pre-school is a carefully prepared environment designed to work hand in hand with the child's "absorbent mind" and "sensitive periods." It's aim is to promote independent learning and exploration by the child.

The prepared environment consists of three elements, the classroom and the children in it, the materials and the specially trained teacher. Each of these elements is incomplete on it's own i.e. the teacher is incomplete without the materials and the classroom and the materials are incomplete without the teacher's guidance on how to use them. The three elements must always work in unison.

The Montessori classroom is a painstakingly prepared environment. It is essentially a "children's house," i.e. a house designed specifically for children, where all the chairs, tables, toilet facilities and sinks are child sized and where all the shelves are low and open so that children can reach everything without having to ask for assistance.

Because it is the children's house they are allowed to move freely within it, selecting activities which interest and attract them as opposed to being made to do something selected by a teacher.

The classroom is a well ordered place answering the young child's desperate need for order and structure. The materials are always kept in the same place each day and the children learn to return them to the same place after use. An ordered environment helps the children to become calm and serene. The classroom usually has distinct areas for the different types of activities - practical life, sensorial, number work, language, culture and art. This is purely for the sake of order, no subject is ever treated in isolation. All subjects are shown to be interrelated.

The classroom is designed to aid in independent learning so that the child, through the use of the materials and with the guidance of the teacher actually teaches himself.

Montessori discovered that this is really the best way for a child under six to learn - by teaching himself through the use of carefully selected materials and with the guidance of a patient and well trained teacher.

6

In a true Montessori school the classroom is a "children's community," and there is a conscious effort to promote a community and family spirit among the children and a sense of responsibility towards each other.

When something spills, the children help each other to clean up. When shelves look dirty, children organise a little group to dust them. When windows need washing (and even when they don't !) there is always one or two ready with a

bucket and sponge. The teacher never commands any child to do anything but gently guides them and helps them to learn how to organise themselves and then allows them to carry out their jobs without interruption.

As the children go about their self chosen tasks in a busy but calm manner, they gradually develop a sense of maturity and family spirit.

The age group in a Montessori class is carefully planned to encourage this family spirit. There are usually three, four and five year olds in the same classroom.

Dr. Montessori stressed that this mixture of ages is crucial to the success of the class. Children need to learn how to get along with others of different ages and abilities. It is a skill which cannot be learned theoretically, it must be practiced on a daily basis.

In a true Montessori classroom, older children have regular opportunities to help younger children with practical things such as doing up their buttons or shoes, and with academic tasks such as learning to count or read. This develops leadership skills as well as patience and kindness in the older child.

Similarly, younger children profit from having the daily stimulation of watching older children doing number work, reading, writing, doing, geography etc. and they become motivated to learn to do these things themselves.

The Montessori Materials

The aim of the Montessori materials is often misunderstood. The materials are not simply meant to teach skills or concepts, they have a much deeper purpose. They aim to awaken the child, to capture his attention and focus his mind, helping him become calm and eventually bringing about a development in his intelligence.

The first thing every child needs to learn is how to concentrate. However no one can teach him how to do this, so he needs materials which bring about concentration. The materials designed by Maria Montessori do exactly this. They are straightforward and uncluttered in design.

If the material deals with colour, then everything in the material is identical in size, shape, weight etc. and differs only in colour.

If the material deals with weight, then everything in the material is identical in colour size, and shape and differs only in weight.

The intention is not just to show the child colours, shapes and sizes as if he had never seen them before, after all, since birth he has been bombarded with colours, shapes and sizes.

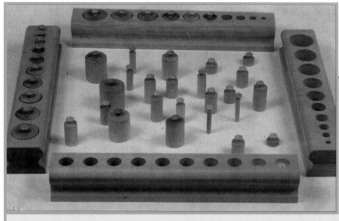

*The intention is rather to show him these things in such a way that his mind begins to see class-*ifications and categories and begins to understand that all things are part of a structure and are not chaotic.

The materials are mostly self correcting so that when a child makes an error, it becomes obvious to him from the material itself that an error has been made e.g. there will be a piece that doesn't match anything else or a piece that doesn't fit into the last slot etc. The child will then have the opportunity to use his own initiative to correct the error.

Dr. Montessori felt that it was crucial that children learn to see error as information, to see it as a vital part of the learning process, not as something to be ashamed of or embarrassed about.

It is much easier for this to happen if the error is pointed out by the material itself rather than by an adult.

The Teacher

When Dr. Montessori discovered how young children actually learn, how they take in the world, not by listening to someone talking about it, but simply by living in it, by experiencing it, by touching, tasting, feeling it, she realised that a new type of teacher was needed.

The Montessori teacher is not the centre of the classroom and she is not the giver of inform-ation. Instead she is the link between the child and the prepared envron-ment of the classroom. The classroom with all its materials is useless to the child without the teacher's guidance.

The Montessori teacher should be a highly trained adult who knows the developmental needs of children, and has the ability to recognise periods of readiness in each individual child. She should be able to judge when to guide a child towards an activity that will be good for him and when to discretely steer him away from an activity that will only frustrate him because he is not ready for it yet.

She should be a keen observer of children and she should have the ability to recognise the individual interests and needs of each child as well as those of the class as a whole. It is her role to make sure that these interests and needs are met and that no child becomes bored or frustrated because the door to the next level of exploration has not been opened for him. Once that door has been opened, the teacher must stand back and only give help when looked for Dr. Montessori always pointed out that any unnecessary help is always a hindrance to development. One of the most important roles of the teacher is that of giving individual presentations, i.e. short lessons on how to use the materials. It is precisely because the children are free to move around and work independently that the teacher is always free to give individual attention to any child as needed or requested.

Above all, since the teacher is to play this vital role as "link" between the child and the prepared environment, she must be someone who is mentally alert and open to life her self. In a sense, it is she who breathes life into the materials and the classroom. It is up to her to create a living environment, in which she shares with the children, the joy of discovery and growth.

Dr. Montessori organised her activities into distinct subject areas as follows:- practical life, sensorial, mathematical, language, art, music and culture.

The child in the class, however, is blissfully unaware of any distinction between subjects and is usually progressing in several areas at the same time.

In each subject area, Dr. Montessori suggested a general sequence for the presenting of activities to each individual child.

The teacher is very conscious of this sequence and takes care to guide a child from one stage to the next so that he is guaranteed to succeed in his learning and so will grow in confidence and self esteem.

All children move through the curriculum at their own pace and are encouraged to develop to their full potential. Most importantly, they are never compared to their classmates.

In a typical class, a three year old may be washing windows or pouring rice from jug to jug.

Alongside him, a four year old may be making up short words and sentences with letters known as the moveable alphabet.

Nearby a four or five year old may be counting spindles (wooden sticks) into boxes and thereby teaching himself about quantity and numerals, while another four or five year old is making up puzzle maps of continents and learning about the animals and people of other countries. In practice, this approach actively prevents comparisons.

Children recognise from the beginning that everyone is different and everyone is good at something. One might describe the Montessori curriculum as being a "hidden" curriculum in the sense that it is there but it is not obtrusive - yet the children move through it and in fact often go way beyond it because no limits are placed on any child. A child can go as far as his interest takes him. A good teacher will always be ready to open the next door of exploration for an eager child to go through.

"Real" tasks in a "real" world

Long before a child even reaches her first birthday she shows signs of wanting to do the things she sees adults doing.

14

Dr. Montessori noticed this great desire in young children to be allowed to be useful members of the real world and so in her first school she offered the children real tasks to perform with real but child sized tools and implements. In fact she called her first school a "children's house" because she allowed the children freedom to conduct most of the chores necessary for the running of the "house" themselves - i.e. cleaning, dusting, polishing, preparing food and washing up etc.

Initially she was quite astonished at the change this freedom with responsibility gave to the children. They became incredibly happy, mature and organised. They relished this opportunity to be useful members of the world and they seemed to really appreciate the sense of dignity this gave them.

Since then, it has become a crucial part of Montessori education to offer the children "practical life" tasks. There are four types of practical life activities available to the child -

- Care of the Self

    Washing hands and face, brushing teeth Combing hair, buttoning, zipping etc.

- Care of the Environment

    Dusting, sweeping, cleaning, polishing etc.

- Development of Social Skills

    As part of the practical life curriculum each child is shown how to respond socially - i.e. how to greet, thank, apologise, excuse oneself etc. and each child is given opportunity to practice these social skills within the classroom anytime she wants to.

- Control of Movement

    Finally, within the practical life curriculum comes the ever popular activity "walking on the line" and the equally popular "silence game." Both of these activities help the child to gain control over her movements.

Making "Sense" Of The World

From the moment a new born baby enters the world, he is literally bombarded with sights, sounds, tastes and smells. Ahead of him lies the enormous task of making sense of all these impressions in order that he may gradually come to an understanding of the world he finds himself in. It is a job that each individual child must do for himself.

To help him in this incredible task, nature has given each child, from birth to six years, a heightened sensitivity to sensorial stimuli. To put it simply the child under six years has a natural and extraordinary ability to learn through his senses.

Recognising this sensitive period for learning through the senses, Dr. Montessori devised materials which aim to help the child to classify and categorise his impressions so that he begins to perceive the order behind the seeming chaos.

The Montessori materials invite the child to touch, manipulate, look at, investigate, listen to, smell, taste, measure, examine, compare, contrast etc. but they do so in a very organised and systematic fashion. Each individual material is meant to help the child's mind to focus on only one particular quality at a time - i.e. length, height, weight, shape, sound, taste or smell. Dr. Montessori carefully designed the materials herself to ensure this "isolation of quality."

The sensorial materials also prepare the child in an indirect way for later skills such as reading, writing, mathematics and music. For example, when the child holds the little knobs on the cylinders and geometric shapes, he is indirectly strengthening the small muscles of his hand in preparation for writing. When he uses the sound boxes to match sounds he is training his ears to distinguish between slight differences in sound and therefore indirectly preparing himself to distinguish between phonemes (i.e. sounds in a language) and pitch in musical notes. As he plays with cylinder blocks, happily putting the various sized cylinders into their respective holes, he is unaware that he is indirectly learning about the mathematical concepts of one to one correspondence and seriation.

The beauty then of the sensorial activities is that they appeal to the child's urge to touch and explore everything. They challenge him to perform specific activities, and they give him feedback on his performance by virtue of the fact that the materials are mostly self correcting.

It is in this way that the sensorial activities take the child another stage forward in his great task of making "sense" of the world.

Mathematical Activities

"One, two, skip a few, ninety nine, a hundred"

Young children love maths !

It may be hard for some adults with their own bad memories of horrible homework and dreaded tests to believe, but it is true, young children love maths. They are not afraid of numbers, indeed they are fascinated by them. Once introduced to numbers in the right way, they can't stop counting, measuring and calculating.

Dr. Maria Montessori was one of the first people to notice the young child's natural mathematical mind. Recognising, of course, that certain mathematical concepts cannot be grasped until a certain age, she still discovered that some mathematical operations come easier to younger children than to older ones. It is all a matter of offering the right material at the right time.

In a true Montessori school, the teacher aims to do just this. Preparation for mathematical activities comes indirectly through the practical life activities with their emphasis on precision, and through many of the sensorial activities which introduce the child to length, height etc. at a sensorial level.

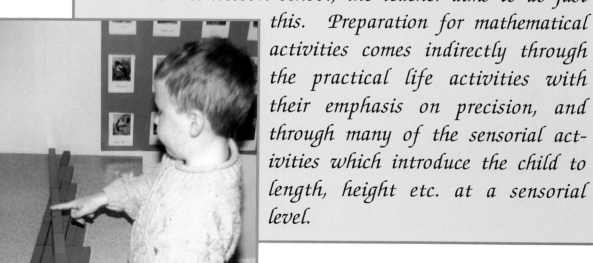

Initially, the children are introduced to number songs, finger play games and other activities which prepare the mind to understand the use of symbols for quantities. Following this, the Montessori mathematics materials are introduced one by one to the children. These are simple, concrete materials which allow the child to "see", "feel", and understand quantities in a very real way. Nothing is abstract at this stage, everything is presented in a concrete fashion for Montessori always pointed out that nothing enters the brain of a young child which hasn't come first of all through the hands. In later years as the child gets older the materials become less and less concrete and move with the child towards abstract thought.

Language Activities

Supercalafragalisticexpialidosious !

Apart from the miracle of birth itself, there can surely be no more extraordinary feat in the young child's life than the learning of language.

Without the aid of language tapes, grammar books or evening classes, the infant teaches herself to distinguish from the host of sounds all around her, what is language and what is background noise.

When she starts to speak, the child doesn't make the sounds of washing machines or telephones or even animal noises, instead she speaks human language.

This is something we take very much for granted, yet if we try to learn a language ourselves or teach a language to an older child, we realise just how difficult a task it is.

Montessori believed that the task of learning language, both spoken and written, was made easier for the child under six by the existence of a "sensitive period" for language learning. She noticed that between birth and six years the child shows a heightened interest in language. We see this in babies when they are just a few months old.

They watch an adult's mouth moving and even put their tiny hands on the adult's lips as he speaks. A month or so later, the baby will begin to make real sounds and she can be heard "practising" these sounds over and over, and so it goes on until the child can speak fluently at about two or three years of age.

In a Montessori classroom, the teacher is very much aware of the child's heightened sensitivity to language and she aims to make the best use of this temporary phase by

making available to the child a wide range of activities which will help the development of both spoken and written language.

Some of these activities involve the use of the traditional Montessori language materials e.g. sandpaper letters, moveable alphabets, metal insets etc. but many of them rely more on songs, stories, finger play games, discussions and opportunities for the children to tell their own news or recount their own experiences.

In most Montessori schools the stories read to children will be about nature, animals or children rather than about fairies or giants. This is because Dr. Montessori always recommended that fairy stories be kept for children over six years who can understand the difference between reality and fantasy.

A unique feature of the Montessori language curriculum is it's interdisciplinary approach. What this means in practice is that as a child uses the Montessori materials for the study of geography, plants, classification of animals and peoples of the world she increases her vocabulary both spoken and written. She learns to recognise and pronounce sight words such as Antarctica, Africa, Australia etc. as well as names of animals and plants. It becomes second nature for her to read and pronounce such words as Siberian tiger, Bactrian camel, European bison etc.

Through this interdisciplinary approach, she learns a most important lesson i.e. that reading is not an end in itself, it is not something you "do" for your homework to please some teacher. It is the key to all further exploration. When a child comes to understand this she will never need any out side encouragement to read books. She will be driven on by her innate curiosity to find out more about the fascinating world she finds herself in.

In Montessori schools, art and music are woven into all curriculum areas. Children learn action songs, number songs, songs  from different countries and cultures, songs about festivals, songs about nature and animals etc. Similarly art activities can take any shape or form that the child chooses. Many children enjoy doing leaf rubbings, paintings, colouring in maps of the world and individual countries. Similarly they often colour in geometric shapes and designs, or simply do freehand drawings.

Art materials, including clay and plasticine are usually freely available to the children. Since Montessori schools recognise that for the child the process is always more important than the finished result, there is very little emphasis  on producing "nice" pictures to bring home to mum and dad. Fancy crafts where ninety percent of the work is done by the teacher have no place in Montessori schools.

Cultural Activities

This Is Our World - The Global Family

"Conservation", "Recycling", Ecology", "Acid Rain", "C.F.C's.", the "Ozone Layer", these have all become household words to us in recent years and for a very serious reason. We have now had to accept that we and the generations before us have endangered the life of the whole planet because of our ignorance and our indifference to the laws of nature.

Over ninety years ago, Dr. Montessori pointed out the importance of bringing up children to be physically and spiritually in contact with nature. She predicted that the destruction of the planet by pollution and waste could not be avoided unless we began to make our children aware of their interdependence with and reliance on nature. Children need to know that one form of life cannot live without another.

In the Montessori school, nature is brought into the classroom. Dr. Montessori designed concrete materials which present the world of nature in such a way that even a three year old can appreciate it. Classifications of the world's animals, plants and land formations (i.e. islands, lakes, peninsulas etc.) studies of the parts of a flower or a tree are presented in simple fashion and in the years to come expanded upon, so that the Montessori child, especially the child who spends several years in a Montessori school becomes an ecologically aware and ecologically responsible adult, which is our only hope for the survival of this planet.

The Tailor-Made School

The Aims And Objectives Of Montessori Schools

What is really unique about Montessori schools is that they are "tailor-made" to suit the needs of the growing child or adolescent.

Dr. Maria Montessori never sat down and invented a method of education to impose on children. Instead she spent a lifetime living and working with children of many different nationalities, colours and creeds, observing them, drawing on her background knowledge of medicine and psychology to help her come to an understanding of their natural drives and needs. Then she developed an educational method to match those needs.

After a lifetime devoted to children Dr. Montessori made the extraordinary and still controversial discovery that no human being can teach another - every person must be their own teacher. The most an adult can do is be a guide, a director, someone who opens the doors of learning for a child to pass through and someone who helps the child to gain the basic tools necessary to be able to teach himself, i.e literacy and numeracy skills. As a result of this discovery, Dr. Montessori realised that what children need is not "institutes of education" where they are force fed with facts and formulas which have no relevance or meaning to them and which are quickly forgotten after exam time, but rather they need learning environments which exactly match their interests and needs at each stage of their development and which nurture their natural, inbuilt desire to learn.

This is what true Montessori schools aim to be. By the time of her death Dr. Montessori had established "tailor-made" communities, not just for the three to six age group but also for the six to nines, the nine to twelves, the twelve to fifteens and the fifteen to eighteens.

The first aim then of Montessori schools is to create environments which match the needs of the children in them rather than expect children to fit into a mould designed by adults to suit adults.

The next aim is to enthuse the hearts and minds of the children so that they become motivated to explore and discover the world they live in and so become life long learners, who pursue knowledge for it's own sake and who study out of a desire to understand more about man and his function and role in the universe. To do this they must first of all become independent, creative and self confident thinkers. It is one of the first objectives of Montessori education to enable children to achieve this independence creativity and self confidence.

The ultimate aim of Montessori education is to create communities where parents, teachers and children work together in harmony, learning to respect and care for each other. Dr. Montessori really believed that this kind of upbringing could lead to a reconstruction of society eventually bringing about world peace. It is no surprise that both Hitler and Mussolini closed her schools and burned her books. Nor is it surprising that Dr. Montessori was nominated three times for the Nobel Peace Prize. All Montessori schools should uphold Dr. Montessori's ultimate aim of bringing about world peace through the meaningful education of our children - the leaders of tomorrow.

- ## The "right" teacher

Up until her death in 1952, Dr. Maria Montessori took every possible step to ensure that every teacher trained in the Montessori method of education reached the standard of excellence demanded by herself. She personally presided over her own training courses until her death at the age of eighty two.

Since her death, many different types of Montessori teacher training courses have sprung up all over the world. Recently, measures have been put in place to standardise and accredit the diverse range of programs which offer certificates and diplomas in Montessori education. While the vast majority of Montessori training colleges are committed to providing training of the highest standard, the reality is that teachers offering Montessori classes to children may have very varied levels of training. For this reason, it would be in the parent's own interest to seek out a school where the teacher is known to be committed to true Montessori principles.

- ## The "right" school

This book has described something of what Montessori schools should be, but in reality since the name "Montessori" is now a generic term, it can be used freely and consequently some schools use the name Montessori simply to attract parents and make money.

They may not necessarily adhere to the principles and practices laid down by Dr. Montessori. For this reason it is vital that parents be well informed and know what it is they are looking for.

In the midst of this, a parents task is made more difficult by the fact that Montessori schools are not like chain stores - they are not all identical. Just as no two families are alike so also each school will differ slightly according to the personality, education, experience and enthusiasm of the teacher. However, there are some elements that should be constant in all Montessori schools and these are what you should look for when you visit a prospective school.

- The room or rooms should contain child sized furniture The seating should cater for both group and individual work. The shelves should be low and open so that children can reach the materials without having to ask for adult assistance.

- There should be a variety of materials present which represent the subject areas - practical life, sensorial, mathematical, language, art, music and cultural.

A word of caution here. Do not be dazzled by the materals alone. Any school can place expensive looking materials on a shelf and give the appearance of being a good school. However, a good school is much more than the materials in it. Remember it is the extent to which Montessori philosophy is applied and practised which makes a school good or bad. There are always a few Montessori schools operating on a small budget, making many of their own materials, and charging modest fees, but where the spirit of real Montessori education is present in everything they do. So pay attention to what the teachers say to you about how they apply Montessori theory and practice in the day to day running of the school.

• There should be a mixture of ages spanning a three year range e.g. there should be three, four and five year olds in a pre-school class. Some schools now separate the three and four year olds into junior and senior Montessori. This practice is wrong and no explanations are acceptable. Dr. Montessori continuously emphasised the crucial importance of having a three year age span in the class. If three year olds do not see four and five year olds reading and doing simple maths then they are deprived of a learning experience which would motivate them to learn to read and do maths themselves.

If four year olds are not in a class with three year olds they will be deprived of an opportunity to be leaders and helpers. They will not develop the same degree of patience and charitable understanding that they would develop if they were in a class with younger children.

• There should be freedom of movement i.e. the children should be free to move around while conducting their self chosen activities. There should be an atmosphere of calm business, e.g. children walking to and from shelves, taking and replacing materials, laying out floor mats, conversing with friends etc. there should not, however, be a loud din as this would lead to chaos and prevent all learning and development.

- *There should be uninterrupted work periods. In the early months, when Dr. Montessori tried to figure out why her classes were so successful, why the children were so happy and were developing so well, she spent many hours just watching the children at work and play. She discovered that when children are allowed to work at something of their own choosing without interruption or interference from adults or other children, they develop an amazing power of concentration. When they finish the task they have been working at (often after repeating it over and over again) they awake as if from a slumber feeling not tired as might be expected, but rejuvenated, alert, joyful, at peace with themselves and ready to socialise with others.*

It is of crucial importance that every Montessori school allow each child to have uninterrupted work cycles. There should be no bells or buzzers or calls to storytime, songtime or any other time if a child is in the middle of concentrated work. It is up to every teacher to protect the child's right to these uninterrupted cycles which are the keys to the child's future development.

- *There should be a parent education program - (even if it only consists of one or two meetings with the parents) designed to inform them about the basics of Montessori philosophy.*

Experience shows that Montessori education works best when parents also apply the principles of Montessori philosophy in their own homes. This aids the development of happy, well balanced children.

Questions Parents Ask

1. **What is the best age for a child to begin Montessori pre-school ?**

   The ideal age for a child to begin Montessori pre-school is between two and a half and three years. However, some children are not emotionally ready to be separated from their parents at this age. If this is the case, the parents should wait until the child is a little older.

2. **Will a child benefit from only one year at a Montessori pre-school or does he need to attend for the whole cycle (i.e. three to six years) to derive any real benefit ?**

   Any time spent in a true Montessori school will benefit a child. However, experience shows that the more years a child spends in the carefully prepared Montessori environment, especially during the sensitive years between birth and six, the more long lasting the impact is on the child's later development.

   Dr. Montessori saw that every child's development falls naturally into cycles of approximately three years - birth to three, three to six, six to nine, etc. up until adulthood. Between three and six years (or roughly around the time the milk teeth start to fall out) every child goes through a period of self construction, in other words, during this time, a child builds the person he is to be. If a child is allowed to spend these years in a true Montessori setting he will benefit enormously. In the first year, the three year old is the junior, laying foundations and learning from the older children. In the second year, he is stable and spends his time building on his foundations and perfecting his skills. In the third year, he is a leader, teaching others younger than himself and re-inforcing his own learning.

3. **How is discipline managed in a Montessori school ?**

   In a true Montessori school discipline is managed by activity - there are no rewards for good behaviour and there are no punishments for bad behaviour. If a child is being difficult, the teacher quickly removes him from the troublesome situation and invites him to carry out an activity which will occupy his body and mind and eventually bring about a positive change in his behaviour.

Montessori schools aim to help every child to develop self discipline. This is why rewards and punishments have no place in the Montessori classroom. At the beginning of the year simple ground rules are explained and every child is encouraged to do the right thing for its own sake. This type of discipline does not develop overnight (despite the fervent prayers of the teacher), it develops gradually as the teacher guides the child through various activities giving him a combination of freedom and responsibility.

Each day, the child gains increased mastery over himself, his moods, his behaviour, until finally he can act unselfishly and maturely taking into account the feelings of others and taking responsibility for his own learning.

4. Does attendance at a Montessori school make all children "bright" or "advanced" for their age ?

No. Montessori education was never about making children "bright" or "advanced". Montessori education is about allowing children to develop at their own pace, following their own interests. It is about giving children an environment in which they can develop independence, self discipline, respect for others, concentration and a love of learning.

However, since the Montessori pre-school classroom is filled with materials of interest to children from two and a half to six or seven years, it frequently happens that many, though certainly not all, children become very advanced by using these materials or even by watching others using them.

It must always be remembered that Montessori schools do not aim to "teach" children, they aim to allow them to learn.

5. How many children should there be in a Montessori pre-school class ?

The answer to this question depends entirely on the size of the building being used and the legal and insurance requirements. The room or rooms should be large enough to allow each child the freedom to carry out his activities in safety and comfort.

There is a common misconception that Montessori schools have always favoured small class sizes and low child/teacher ratios. This is not actually true. Historically, Montessori schools were often very large ones with around forty pupils to a class with only one teacher and sometimes one helper in attendance.

Yet the results of these early schools were astonishing and in fact, much more noteworthy than anything we hear of nowadays. The great success of these early schools was actually due to the combination of their large number, their mixture of ages and their adherence to true Montessori principles and practices. In these large schools, older children were allowed to teach younger ones, and the school was a stable community because only the oldest third moved out of the class each year making room for the new, younger children.

Nowadays, because of the public obsession with small class sizes and low pupilteacher ratios, many Montessori schools have been forced to operate very small classes. This is unfortunate because in a very small class the teacher may dominate, even, unintentionally. The children may feel the presence of the teacher very strongly and become inhibited and show less initiative than they would in a larger, busier class. Also the children may have fewer opportunities to see the materials being used by older children as the number of older children in the class will be minimal.

When it comes to class size and pupil/teacher ratio, the safety of each child should be paramount and the legal and insurance requirements must be met but there should be no domination of adults.

6. **How do children settle in traditional state schools after their Montessori experience ?**

This varies from child to child and from school to school. All children are adaptable and after an initial settling in period, they usually get used to their new school and it's different approach. The child from a Montessori pre-school will usually have developed independence, self discipline, initiative, motivation, a love of learning, respect for others and a capacity to work at things without constant supervision. All of these traits should be of great benefit to any child in any type of school.

7. **Can a method which was invented nearly a hundred years ago still have relevance today ?**

Yes it can and for very specific reasons. As stated earlier, Dr. Maria Montessori's ideas were very much ahead of her time and to a great extent, modern early education specialists are only "catching up" with them. When Dr. Montessori presented her ideas, based on her observations of children, she could not prove them scientifically, although she felt certain of them intuitively. The difference today is that the most current brain development research is now confirming many of Dr. Montessori's observations.

Montessori stated boldly that her observations showed that the child under six had an "absorbent mind" and that he was capable of absorbing knowledge, language and culture effortlessly from his surrounding environment simply by living in it and consequently, the environment we provide for a child under six must be very carefully prepared. Nowadays, no early childhood specialist would dispute the fact that approximately half of the child's mental development occurs before he reaches his fourth birthday and over three quarters of his mental development occurs before he is eight years old.

In the light of this knowledge, Dr. Montessori's emphasis on the importance of the type of environment we provide for the child in his formative years has great relevance today and will continue to have relevance for as long as human beings continue to exist.

Common Criticisms Of Montessori Schools

1. **Some Montessori teachers have a superior "know it all" attitude which is off putting both to parents and to others working in mainstream or play-school education.**

   Unfortunately, this is all too true of some Montessori teachers and it is something that the major training colleges should start to examine. None of us hold a monopoly on knowledge and there is much to be gained by the exchange of ideas. This does not mean that we must water down or part with our cherished principles but we must avoid tunnel vision. In the complex area of child development no one system can hold all the answers.

2. **Children have too much freedom in Montessori schools - they can do whatever they feel like doing, whenever they feel like doing it.**

   This is not actually true, but one can see how this misunderstanding of what really goes on in a Montessori classroom could come about.

   First of all the Montessori classroom is a "prepared environment", this means that the teacher has carefully selected every stick of material that is in the room. She has discarded anything that would be superflous and only kept the things which are beneficial to the child in the room. Therefore she can allow the child to choose freely from what is available because his choices have already been curtailed for him by the teacher, for his own good. The only time a child would not be allowed to use something is when the teacher feels that he has chosen something too advanced for his present stage of development which would only frustrate and annoy him. In a case like this, the teacher would offer the child an alternative activity.

   What the child experiences is, in effect, a freedom within limits. It is freedom not license. He is free to do anything which is good, useful, productive, but he is not free to do anything which is bad, useless, wasteful or destructive.

36

3. *Children are given no freedom in Montessori schools. They have to do activities exactly as the teacher shows them - there is no room for innovation or creativity.*

This is again untrue, (although one has heard horror stories of some very rigid so called Montessori schools where very strict and incorrect interpretations of Montessori principles has led to very rigid practices) and one or two visits to real Montessori schools would dispel these fears. Children in Montessori schools are certainly not prevented from being innovative or creative, but they are stopped from misusing materials.

There are two kinds of materials in the Montessori classroom - ordinary pre-school materials and specially manufactured Montessori materials. Most of the Montessori materials have a specific purpose, e.g. they aim to draw the child's attention to a particular quality e.g. colour, dimension, number etc. and a child is shown briefly what that purpose is and then invited to work or play with the material to discover it's uses for himself. Often children will discover many innovative and creative uses of the materials. If, however, the child starts to misuse the material (e.g. by using a number rod as a sword or a baton) the teacher would intervene and either show the child the correct use of the material again or offer something else. The teacher would be careful not to offend the child and would simply and casually say that the material isn't used in that way.

There is nothing wrong with this approach. No parent would dream of giving their three year old an electric kettle to be used as a watering can, or a good compact disc to be used as a frisbie, so too the Montessori teacher will not allow a child to use material for the wrong purpose. If the teacher allows misuse of the material, she deprives the child of gaining the benefit that the material was designed to give.

Within the Montessori classroom, there are so many different activities available that the child has and always should have plenty of scope for creative and innovative play.

4. *Children are not allowed to socialise in Montessori schools, they do all their activities on their own and do not learn to mix with other children.*

Anyone who has ever visited a real Montessori school would laugh aloud at this criticism because the very opposite is true. However many people, especially primary school teachers who have never spent time in Montessori schools still hold this view.

The explanation for this fallacy lies in the misleading way Montessori philosophy has been handed down in the history of education textbooks, often written by people who have never set foot in a Montessori classroom.

An example of this misinformation occurred recently when this author's own husband, while visiting a major resource centre for teachers found that the only book on Montessori education available for primary school teachers using the centre was the now outdated criticism of her work written by William Heard Kilpatrick and published in 1912.

None of the many excellent books which have recently been written about Montessori education, e.g. John Chattin McNichols "The Montessori Controversy," or Paula Polk Lillard's "Montessori Today," were available, nor were they even listed in the bibliographies. Why this total disregard for and wilful ignorance of Montessori education?

Children in a real Montessori school are part of a community. There is a family spirit. The children develop a very caring attitude towards each other. The mixture of ages encourages the children to help each other. This socialisation is one of the cornerstones of Montessori philosophy.

This misunderstanding arises as a result of the emphasis on individual activity in Montessori classrooms. Children in Montessori classrooms are initially encouraged to choose their own activity and they work away parallel to other children. In reality, children relish this opportunity for individual activity. It seems to answer a need they have to be independent and to work at something without the threat of interference from others. They relish the opportunity to be allowed to complete something all by themselves. They develop pride of achievement.

As they get older, towards four years, children begin to enjoy working with other children and sharing tasks. Every child should be allowed to go through this period of self-construction when he desires to do things for himself without interference from adults or other children. It is through this period of individual activity that the child builds himself up and eventually makes himself ready to become a useful member of the group at large with something of his own to contribute. We should respect this valid stage in a child's life when individual activity is so important to him and we should not be so obsessed with socialisation. Socialisation comes naturally, in it's own time. If we force it, we are making the mistake of putting the cart before the horse, and that can only lead to disaster.

Helpful books on Montessori

Title	Author
The Secret Of Childhood	Dr. Maria Montessori
The Absorbent Mind	Dr. Maria Montessori
The Discovery Of The Child	Dr. Maria Montessori
Montessori Play And Learn	Lesley Britton
Teaching Montessori In The Home (The Pre-School Years)	Elizabeth Hainstock
Teaching Montessori In The Home (The School Years)	Elizabeth Hainstock
The Essential Montessori	Elizabeth Hainstock
Montessori In The Classroom	Paula Polk Lillard
Montessori: A Modern Approach	Paula Polk Lillard
Montessori Today	Paula Polk Lillard
The Montessori Controversy	John Chattin McNichols

Useful Addresses

Address	E-mail and web site
American Montessori Society 281 Park Avenue South (6th Floor) New York N.Y. 10010-6102 U.S.A.	AMSPaul@aol.com AMSMichael@aol.com www.amshq.com
AMS Contact address in Ireland	
American Montessori Society C/O The Liberties Vocational School Bull Alley Dublin 8 Ireland	
The Montessori Foundation 901 North Pitt Street Alexandria 22314 Virginia U.S.A.	timseldin@aol.com www.montessori.org
London Montessori Centre 18 Balderton Street London W1Y ITG U.K.	lmc@montessori.ac.uk www.montessori.ac.uk
International Montessori Society 912 Thayer Avenue 207 Silver Spring Maryland 20910 U.S.A.	havis@erols.com www.wdn.com/trust/ims